CW00554206

BACKSTAGE

MERCEDES-BENZ FASHION WEEK BERLIN

Claudius Holzmann

teNeues

BACKSTAGE WIRD DIE SHOW ERSCHAFFEN

Als IMG im Jahr 2007 begann, die Mercedes-Benz Fashion Week Berlin auszurichten, war es unser Ziel, das glamouröseste Mode-Event Deutschlands zu etablieren. Berlin hatte auf der Liste der Modehauptstädte schon in den 1920er Jahren einen der oberen Plätze eingenommen. Doch infolge des Zweiten Weltkriegs und der deutschen Teilung hatte sich die Mode- und Textilbranche bis zur Wiedervereinigung 1990 über das ganze Land verteilt.

Im Lauf der 1990er Jahre wurde mit dem Entstehen und Aufstieg neuer Marken und Designunternehmen eines immer offensichtlicher: In Deutschland fehlte eine Plattform, auf der sich diese Labels einem internationalen Publikum präsentieren konnten. Die einzige Stadt, die das Zielpublikum, die Profis aus der Branche, ansprechen konnte – das war von Anfang an unstrittig –, war Berlin. Die Hauptstadt hatte sich zum kreativen Zentrum im Herzen Europas gemausert und war daher dazu angetan, das Interesse der Medien, der Kunden und der Meinungsmacher aus aller Welt zu wecken. Mercedes-Benz, die renommierte Marke mit ihrem außergewöhnlichen Engagement in der Modebranche, konnte als Hauptsponsor für die Veranstaltung gewonnen werden, die sich mittlerweile zur weltweit anerkannten Modewoche entfaltet hat. Auch Sponsoren wie DHL und Maybelline Jade tragen erheblich zum Erfolg der Mercedes-Benz Fashion Week Berlin bei.

Modenschauen und die zweimal jährlich stattfindenden Modewochen sind aus der Branche nicht mehr wegzudenken. Hier haben Designer Gelegenheit, ihre Visionen für die nächste Saison zu präsentieren und die Insider und Fachleute der Branche unmittelbar zu erreichen.

Der Raum hinter der Bühne ist erfüllt von Emotionen – Lachen wie Weinen. Hier verwandeln sich Mädels und Jungs von nebenan in Ikonen der Schönheit. Backstage wird die Show erschaffen, es ist der betriebsamste und gleichsam intimste Arbeitsbereich der Kreativen. Das Buch, das Sie in der Hand haben, gewährt Ihnen einen exklusiven Blick hinter die Kulissen und bringt Ihnen die spannende Backstage-Atmosphäre einer Modenschau nach Hause. Sie tauchen in die emotionsgeladene Atmosphäre ein, erleben die Perfektion eines professionellen Make-ups und die schwer definierbare Faszination des neu geschaffenen Modelooks, der auf dem Laufsteg von Hunderten von Fotografen festgehalten und an die Medien rund um den Globus geschickt wird.

Ich wünschte Ihnen viel Freude an diesem Ausflug an den faszinierendsten und glamourösesten Ort der Modebranche – den Backstage-Bereich hinter den Kulissen der Mercedes-Benz Fashion Week Berlin.

Maia Guarnaccia
Vice President, IMG Fashion, Europe

BACKSTAGE IS WHERE IT ALL COMES TOGETHER

When IMG started organizing Mercedes-Benz Fashion Week Berlin in 2007, we were determined to establish one of the most glamorous fashion events in Germany. Berlin was already considered one of the top fashion capitals in the 1920s, but because of the Second World War and the political circumstances of East and West Germany, the German fashion and textile industry dissipated all over the country at the time of the reunification in 1990.

As emerging brands and designer companies grew and expanded throughout the 1990s, it became more and more obvious that in all of Germany there was no platform where these labels could present their work to an international audience. One thing was clear from the beginning: the only place that would attract the right target group of industry professionals was Berlin. Berlin had turned into a creative center in the very heart of Europe that would be able to catch the attention of the press, buyers and opinion leaders from all around the world. Mercedes-Benz, the prestigious brand with a one-of-a-kind engagement in fashion, became the title sponsor for an event that now has grown into a globally recognized fashion week. Additionally, sponsors like DHL and Maybelline Jade contribute tremendously to the success of Mercedes-Benz Fashion Week Berlin.

The fashion show, and its twice yearly exhibition during fashion weeks, is one of the most significant elements of the fashion industry. This is where the designer gets to present their vision for the next season and place their messages with fashion insiders and industry experts.

Backstage is a room full of emotion, a space where you see the laughter and the tears and the miraculous event of models turning from girl- or boy-next-door into a canvas of beauty and looks. Backstage is where it all comes together; it is indeed the designer's busiest and most intimate space. The book you are holding in your hands grants you an exclusive look behind the scenes and brings the excitement of a fashion show's backstage into your home. You will experience the emotion, the exquisiteness of perfect make-up, and the elusive attraction of the finished look that will be photographed by over a hundred photographers, who send their catwalk images to the media around the globe.

I hope you will enjoy the trip into one of the most fascinating, glamorous places within the fashion industry, backstage of Mercedes-Benz Fashion Week Berlin.

Maia Guarnaccia
Vice President, IMG Fashion, Europe

Mercedes-Benz
FASHIONWEEK
BERLIN 2010

DER SPIRIT VON BERLIN

Mein Weg nach Berlin war lang. Ich hatte zwar in den letzten Jahren in Berlin schon gezeigt, aber die Zweifel an Berlin als Fashion-Metropole waren groß. Zuviel Tristesse, zu wenig Glamour, zu grau. Zum Glück nur Vorurteile – im Sommer 2009 änderte ich meine Meinung schlagartig. Meine Show auf der Mercedes-Benz Fashion Week Berlin war ein „Kracher". Die begehrten Chefredakteurinnen der Modepresse, die großen Tageszeitungen – alle waren da! Die Promiriege in der ersten Reihe „unendlich" lang, von Jessica Schwarz bis zum Hollywood-Glanz mit Diane Kruger. Blitzlichtgewitter, Komplimente ohne Ende. Ich war im Taumel und bin seitdem überzeugt: Berlin hat das Zeug mit Paris, Mailand und London in einer Reihe zu stehen. Die Stimmung in der Stadt, die Begeisterung der unzähligen Fashion-Freaks, Presserummel, Stars und Sternchen und nicht zuletzt die Einkäufer lassen Berlin zu *dem* Mode-Event werden. Meine Umsätze gingen steil nach oben – trotz Krise.

Der Spirit von Berlin macht's möglich. Berlin ist Fashion – ich bin froh, dabei zu sein.

THE SPIRIT OF BERLIN

The road to Berlin was a long one for me. I had indeed already shown my designs in Berlin in recent years, but I still had great doubt in Berlin as a fashion capital: too much dreariness, too little glamour, too gray. Luckily, these were only preconceptions. In the summer of 2009, I abruptly changed my opinion. My show at the Mercedes-Benz Fashion Week Berlin was a "hit." The hottest editors in chief in the fashion press, the big daily newspapers—they were all there! The list of celebrities in the first row was "infinitely" long, from Jessica Schwarz to Diane Kruger with her Hollywood glamour. A flurry of camera flashes and endless compliments, I was reeling and have been convinced ever since that Berlin has what it takes to be included in the ranks of Paris, Milan and London. The city's atmosphere, the enthusiasm of the countless fashion freaks, the press hype, the stars and starlets, and—last but not least—the buyers all make Berlin a real fashion event. My sales went up dramatically despite the economic crisis.

It's the spirit of Berlin that makes it possible. Berlin is fashion. I'm happy to be a part of it.

Anja Gockel

DIE TAUFE MEINER KOLLEKTION

Berlin steckt sicher noch in den Kinderschuhen, aber es ist sehr beachtlich, was hier in so kurzer Zeit erreicht worden ist. Ein hohes Maβ an Professionalität, Organisation und Hingabe erwartet einen jede Saison aufs Neue, wenn der Fashion-Wahnsinn am Bebelplatz einzieht. Was IMG, Mercedes-Benz und andere Partner leisten, ist für uns Berliner Designer eine Plattform, dessen Wichtigkeit sich immer fester verankert.

Durch die Mercedes-Benz Fashion Week Berlin haben wir die Gelegenheit, auf deutsche Mode aufmerksam zu machen. Wir bekommen die Möglichkeit, uns einem immer internationaler werdenden Publikum in einem wahnsinnig professionellen Umfeld zu präsentieren. Dass Suzy Menkes letzte Saison bei den Shows zu Gast war, zeigt doch, dass sich hier keiner mehr verstecken muss.

Im Januar 2010 werde ich meine vierte MBFWB-Show in Folge haben. Das ist für mich jedes Mal etwas ganz besonderes. Diese Momente dort, die Stimmung, das ist einzigartig. Für mich als Designer ist die Mercedes-Benz Fashion Week Berlin jede Saison wie die Taufe meiner Kollektion.

THE BAPTISM OF MY COLLECTION

Berlin is surely still in its infancy but what has been achieved here in such a short time is indeed very remarkable. Every season, a high degree of professionalism, organization and dedication await us anew when fashion madness takes over Bebelplatz. IMG, Mercedes-Benz and other sponsors give Berlin designers a platform, the significance of which becomes clearer all the time.

The Mercedes-Benz Fashion Week Berlin gives us the chance to make people aware of German fashion. We get the opportunity to introduce ourselves to an increasingly international audience in a highly professional environment. The fact that Suzy Menkes was a guest at the shows last season shows that no one has to hide here anymore.

In January 2010, I will have my fourth MBFW show in a row and each time it is always something very special for me. The moments there, the atmosphere—they are truly unique. For me as a designer, the Mercedes-Benz Fashion Week Berlin is like the baptism of my collection every season.

Kilian Kerner

{DESIGNER for TOMORROW}

In Juli 2010 findet der Nachwuchsaward „Designer for Tomorrow" zum dritten Mal im Rahmen der Mercedes-Benz Fashion Week Berlin statt. Acht Newcomer präsentieren dabei jeweils fünf Kollektionsteile, die von einer renommierten Jury bewertet werden. Dem Sieger oder der Siegerin winken ein Preisgeld und ein individuelles Förderprogramm. Dazu gehören unterschiedliche Bausteine wie Info- und Produktionsreisen, Insider-Gespräche, PR-Unterstützung oder auch die Umsetzung einer eigenen Modenschau auf der nächsten Fashion Week wie bei Sam Frenzel, dem Gewinner der letzten Saison.

Mit seiner Kollektion „nuit blanche" konnte Sam Frenzel im vergangenen Jahr die meisten Stimmen der Jury auf sich vereinigen. Viele Artikel und Editorials in internationalen Zeitungen und Magazinen wie der *New York Times*, der *Vogue*, der *Cosmopolitan* und der *Marie Claire* waren die Konsequenz dieses Erfolgs. Als besonders positiv empfand Frenzel, dass er durch den Sieg seine Arbeit nach außen tragen und die positive Reaktion seiner Umwelt erleben konnte: „Vor allem die Frauen waren begeistert. Das ist mir am Wichtigsten, da ich ja für sie designe."

Die Frauen tragen die Mode nicht nur, einige bewerten sie auch. So wie *InStyle*-Chefredakteurin Annette Weber, die bereits zum wiederholten Mal als Jurorin im Boot sitzt. Denn ihr gefällt, dass der Schwerpunkt der Mercedes-Benz Fashion Week Berlin auf deutscher Mode liegt. Außerdem sei der Award ausgesprochen professionell organisiert und ein seriöses Forum, das den Werdegang der Teilnehmer auch nach der Modewoche weiterverfolge. „Auch die *InStyle* befördert den Werdegang, indem wir fortwährend mit den jungen Designern in Kontakt stehen und deren Mode auch im Heft veröffentlichen", so Weber.

Um Nachhaltigkeit geht es auch dem Initiator des „Designer

In July 2010 the young talent award "Designer for Tomorrow" will be presented at the Mercedes-Benz Fashion Week Berlin for the third year. Each year eight newcomers present five pieces from their collections to be judged by a renowned jury. The winner receives a cash prize and a tailor-made sponsoring program. This may include information and production trips, conversations with insiders, PR support or even the presentation of your own fashion show at the next fashion week—just like last season's winner, Sam Frenzel.

With his "nuit blanche" collection, Sam Frenzel was able to capture the most jury votes last year. This success resulted in many articles and editorial features in international newspapers and magazines such as the *New York Times*, *Vogue*, *Cosmopolitan*, and *Marie Claire*. What Frenzel found particularly beneficial was the fact that, as a result of the win, he was able to show his work to the rest of the world and experience the positive reaction of his audience. "The women were particularly enthusiastic. They are the most important to me since they are the ones I design for."

Women not only wear fashion; some of them also rate it, like German *InStyle* Editor-in-Chief Annette Weber, who is serving as a juror once again because she likes the fact that the Mercedes-Benz Fashion Week Berlin focuses on German fashion. The award is also known to be a professionally organized and serious forum which continues to have a positive impact on the participant's career even after the fashion week. "*InStyle* also promotes careers by constantly keeping in touch with young designers. We also publish their designs in the magazine," says Weber.

Lasting success is also important to the initiator of the

DfT
ESIGNER for
OMORROW

DESIGNER for TOMORROW

TOMORRO

Ob New York, Paris, London, Mailand oder Berlin: die Fashion Week ist das Highlight der Modebranche. Die angesagtesten Designer zeigen hier die aktuellen Kollektionen der nächsten Saison und setzen Akzente für kommende Trends. Doch nicht nur Farben, Stoffe und Schnitte, sondern auch der Look wird inspiziert und gefeiert. Dazu gehören natürlich das entsprechende Hairstyling und der passende Make-up Look. Ohne diesen wäre die Mode unvollständig – und umgekehrt. Das Ergebnis: Ein Look, der verrückt, elegant, dezent, schrill, auf jeden Fall individuell ist!

Bereits seit Beginn ist Maybelline Jade offizieller Partner der Mercedes-Benz Fashion Week Berlin in Sachen Make-up. Unter der Leitung von Boris Entrup als Head of Make-up & Styling arbeitet ein über 20-köpfiges Team an Make-up Artisten mit Designern, Agenturen und Models zusammen, um den passenden Look für den jeweiligen Designer zu entwickeln. Eine bewährte Partnerschaft, die beiden Seiten Vorteile bringt. Jungdesigner ebenso wie bekannte Größen profitieren von dem professionellen Make-up und Maybelline Jade umgekehrt von der Inspiration und der Kreativität der Designer. Nicht selten fließen Looks, die auf der Fashion Week entstehen, auch in die kommerziell erhältlichen Looks der Marke mit ein.

In Lookproben einige Wochen vor den Fashion Shows wird das Make-up mit den Designern entwickelt und gestaltet. Aber erst danach geht es für das Make-up Team so richtig los, denn dann finden die Looktrainings statt, in denen die Make-up Artisten die Make-up Looks der Designer erlernen. Wenn erst mal die erste Show der Fashion Week angelaufen ist, ist keine Zeit mehr zu üben. Backstage mischen sich professionelle Routine mit treibender Kreativität und Zeitdruck. Jedes Model will in time geschminkt und gestylt sein, um kurz darauf den neuesten Look auf dem Catwalk zu präsentieren. Doch Boris Entrup und das Maybelline Jade Visagisten-Team bringt so schnell nichts aus der Ruhe. Das Team ist aufgeregt, aber eingespielt und professionell.

Die Models sind oft die ersten, die neue Make-up Produkte dem Härtetest unterziehen. Bessere Umstände könnte man sich nicht vorstellen. Denn wenn das Make-up auf dem Catwalk hält, dann auch im täglichen Einsatz. Viele der Laufsteg-Looks lassen sich zuhause leicht nachmachen, und darum steckt auch immer ein wenig Fashion Week in vielen der Maybelline Jade Produkte.

So setzt die Mercedes-Benz Fashion Week zweimal im Jahr nicht nur aufregende neue Modetrends, sondern auch Akzente in Sachen Make-up. Eine Liaison von Fashion und Make-up, wie sie schöner nicht sein könnte.

Whether New York, Paris, London, Milan or Berlin, fashion week is a highlight for the fashion industry. The hottest designers show their latest collections for the next season and set the course for coming trends. However, it is not just the colors, fabrics and cuts that are viewed and celebrated, but also the look itself. Of course, this includes the look of the hairstyles and make-up. Without them, fashion would be incomplete—and vice versa. The result is a look that is crazy, elegant, restrained, flashy—and always individual!

Since the beginning, Maybelline Jade has been the official partner of the Mercedes-Benz Fashion Week Berlin regarding make-up. Under the direction of Boris Entrup as Head of Make-up & Styling, a team of over 20 make-up artists work together with designers, agencies and models to develop the right look for each designer. A partnership proven to be good for both sides. Young designers as well as well-known big names benefit from the professional make-up, and Maybelline Jade does as well from the designer's inspiration and creativity. It is not uncommon for looks that are created during fashion week to make their way into the brand's commercially available looks.

In look samples a few weeks before the fashion shows, the make-up is developed and created with the designers. Only after that do things really get going for the make-up team because that's when the look training sessions take place where the make-up artists learn the make-up looks of the designer. Once the first show of fashion week starts, there is no more time to practice. Backstage professional routines mix with driven creativity and the pressure of time. Every model wants to be made up and styled in time to present the latest look on the catwalk. Yet Boris Entrup and the Maybelline Jade team of make-up artists remain calm. The team is nervous but well-rehearsed and professional.

Models are often the first to put new make-up products to the test. It is hard to imagine better conditions for it. Because if the make-up holds up on the catwalk, then it will hold up in daily use, too. Many of the runway looks can easily be achieved at home. That's why there is always a little bit of fashion week hidden in many of the Maybelline Jade products.

Therefore, the Mercedes-Benz Fashion Week not only sets exciting new fashion trends twice a year, but also make-up trends. A love affair between fashion and make-up that couldn't be any more beautiful.

MIT ALLEN MITTELN SPIELEN

INTERVIEW MIT BORIS ENTRUP, MAKE-UP ARTIST VON MAYBELLINE JADE UND HEAD OF MAKE-UP & STYLING DER MERCEDES-BENZ FASHION WEEK BERLIN

Herr Entrup, seit 2007 sind Sie als exklusiver Make-up Artist von Maybelline Jade ebenfalls Head of Make-up & Styling der Mercedes-Benz Fashion Week Berlin. Wie beurteilen Sie die Entwicklung der Modewoche in diesen Jahren?

Seit 2007 ist eine Menge passiert, die Mercedes-Benz Fashion Week Berlin hat sich als wichtiges Ereignis der Modebranche in Berlin etabliert. Hat man am Anfang noch etwas experimentiert und improvisiert, ist aus ihr ein professionelles Ereignis für die Branche geworden. Jede Saison kommen neue Designer hinzu, internationale Brands mischen sich mit bereits bekannten, aber auch mit Newcomer-Labels aus Deutschland. Und die Veranstaltung wird von den Medien nun auch ganz anders begleitet und wahrgenommen.

Stellen die beiden Modewochen Highlights in Ihrem Jahr dar? Inwieweit unterscheidet sich die Ihre Arbeit bei der Fashion Week von Ihrer sonstigen Jobs als Make-up Artist?

Für Schauen diesen Ausmaßes arbeiten zu können, und dann noch als Head of Make-up, das ist ganz sicher ein Highlight. Als Verantwortlicher für eine Vielzahl unterschiedlicher Designer in der ersten Reihe zu stehen, ist jedes Mal wieder eine Herausforderung. Bei anderen Jobs stehe ich nicht so sehr im Vordergrund und arbeite einfach vor mich hin. Besonders wenn es nicht um Laufstegschauen geht, arbeitet man viel mehr am Detail und innerhalb eines ganz anderen Zeitrahmens. Für den Laufsteg muss es schnell gehen und trotzdem umwerfend aussehen. Man arbeitet mit einem vielköpfigen Team, alle Models müssen auf den Punkt fertig sein und dabei einen durchgängigen Look pro Designer haben. Kurz vor dem Beginn der Show geht es da schon mal hoch her.

Entwickeln Sie das Styling zusammen mit den Modedesignern und Hair-Stylisten? Treten diese mit konkreten Vorstellungen an Sie heran?

Im Vorfeld geben die Designer per Questionaire bereits Ihre Vorstellungen und Anforderungen bekannt. In diesem Fragebogen steht dann bereits, wie viele Outfits und Models gestylt werden müssen. Oft liegen konkrete Moodcharts oder Fotos bei: Welche Vorstellung des Looks der Designer hat, wie die Kollektion aussieht und welche Sonderanforderungen – wie zum Beispiel Fake Lashes, Applikationen von Steinchen oder anderen Materialien – gewünscht werden. Daraufhin wird man kreativ und macht dem Designer in einer Lookprobe einige Tage vor den Shows, manchmal aber auch erst kurz vor den Shows, Vorschläge. Man erarbeitet sich dann gemeinsam den Look. Der wird per Foto und Skribble festgehalten – mit Anmerkungen welche Produkte/Texturen für welche Details genommen werden – und dann mit dem Team trainiert, damit es für die Show dann reibungslos klappt.

Für wie viele Designer sind Sie in Berlin tätig und wie viele Make-up Artisten arbeiten mit Ihnen zusammen?

In der Sommersaison 2009 waren es über 30 Designer und wir haben in zwei versetzt arbeitenden Make-up Teams mit zusammen 15 Make-up Artisten über 700 Models geschminkt.

Wie viel Zeit haben Sie für das Make-up einer einzelnen Show. Wie sind die typischen Abläufe vor der Show?

Für das gesamte Styling, also Hair- & Make-up aller Models – bei einer Show laufen zwischen 15 und 30 Models – rechnet man drei Stunden. Es hängt davon ab, wie viele Outfits der Designer zeigt und wie oft er die einzelnen Models laufen lässt. Erst werden die Haare gemacht, dann das Make-up, sehr oft ist auch Maniküre, für Sommerkollektionen auch Pediküre notwendig. Am Schluss sind die Heads of Hair und Make-up noch mal für ein Final Checkup gefragt. Spezielle Sondereffekte, wie zum Beispiel superglossy Lippen, werden unmittelbar vor dem Auftritt des Models gemacht.

Bietet Ihnen die Mercedes-Benz Fashion Week Berlin die Möglichkeit zu experimentieren, neue Looks und Produkte auszuprobieren?

Das hängt sehr stark von den Vorstellungen des Designers ab. Ausprobieren ist vielleicht auch nicht das richtige Wort, das klingt mir zu vage. Es zählt die Erfahrung, das Können und die Kreativität bei der Anwendung der Produkte und Materialien. Unsere Produkte von Maybelline Jade kennen wir natürlich sehr gut, denn wir arbeiten ständig damit. Der richtige Ausdruck ist vielleicht, dass wir mit allen Mitteln spielen, um bestimmte Effekte zu erzielen.

USING EVERYTHING IMAGINABLE

INTERVIEW MIT BORIS ENTRUP, MAKE-UP ARTIST FOR MAYBELLINE JADE AND HEAD OF MAKE-UP & STYLING FOR MERCEDES-BENZ FASHION WEEK BERLIN

Mr. Entrup, as exclusive make-up artist for Maybelline Jade, you have also been the Head of Make-up & Styling for Mercedes-Benz Fashion Week Berlin since 2007. What do you think about the development of fashion week over the years?

A lot has happened since 2007; Mercedes-Benz Fashion Week Berlin has established itself as an important event for the fashion industry in Berlin. What began as an improvisational experiment has now become a professional event in the industry. Every season we get more new designers. International brands get mixed with already well-known designers as well as up-and-coming labels from Germany. Also, the event is now being followed by the media and is perceived completely differently.

Are the two fashion weeks the highlights of your year? How much does your work for the fashion week differ from your other jobs as a make-up artist?

To be able to work for shows of this magnitude, and as Head of Make-up, is most definitely a highlight. To be the person responsible for a huge number of different designers is always a challenge. With my other jobs I am not in the spotlight as much and just simply do my work. When I'm not working at runway shows, I concentrate much more on the details and work within a completely different time frame. With runways you have to work fast and the models still need to look absolutely gorgeous. You work with a large team. All of the models have to be ready on time and have a consistent look for each designer. There's a lot of rushing and chaos just before the show begins.

Do you develop the styles together with the fashion designers and hair stylists? Do they come to you with concrete ideas?

The designers give us their ideas and requirements early on in a questionnaire. They have already specified how many outfits and models will have to be styled. The questionnaires often include actual mood charts or photos specifying how the designer imagines the look should be, what the collection looks like and what special requirements, such as fake lashes, applications of stones or other materials, are needed. A few days before the shows we get creative and give the designers suggestions for a sample look. Sometimes it is right before the shows. We then work together on the look. It is documented in photos and notes—with comments on which products/textures will be used for which details—and then practiced with the team so that it works smoothly for the show.

How many designers do you work for in Berlin and how many make-up artists work with you?

In the summer of 2009 there were over 30 designers, and we had two teams with a total of 15 make-up artists, with each team working staggered rotations to make up over 700 models.

How much time do you have for make-up for a single show? What are the typical steps before the show?

We estimate that it takes three hours for the entire styling of a single show which means hair and make-up for all 15 to 30 models. It depends on how many outfits the designer is showing and how often he has the individual models walking the runway. The hair is done first, then the make-up, very often manicures and, for the summer collections, also pedicures. At the end, the Heads of Hair and Make-up are called in for a final check-up. Special effects, such as extremely glossy lips, are added right before the model steps onto the runway.

Does Mercedes-Benz Fashion Week Berlin give you the chance to experiment and try out new looks and products?

That depends a lot on the designers' ideas. "Try out" is, perhaps, not the right term. It sounds too vague to me. What are important are experience, expertise and creativity in the use of the products and materials. We are, of course, very familiar with our Maybelline Jade products because we work with them constantly. Perhaps the right way to say it is that we are using everything imaginable to create specific effects.

NEW YORK
MAYBELLINE
Jade

ORÉAL

MODE
IST EIN
SCHÖNER
MAYBELLINE
NEW YORK
Jade

NEW YORK

NEW

anja gockel
london

REDKEN

2010
GEMEINSAM

JULE

SONY

ORM
52
53
62
63
64

Theresa
Dalia
Nicole
52
50
51
Lukas
Theresa
Natalya
Nicole
61
62
63
64
Nicole
Dalia
74
72
Renata
Zoe
90

KEIN
DURCHGANG
ENTRY

YORK

Mercedes-Benz
FASHIONWEEK
BERLIN 2009

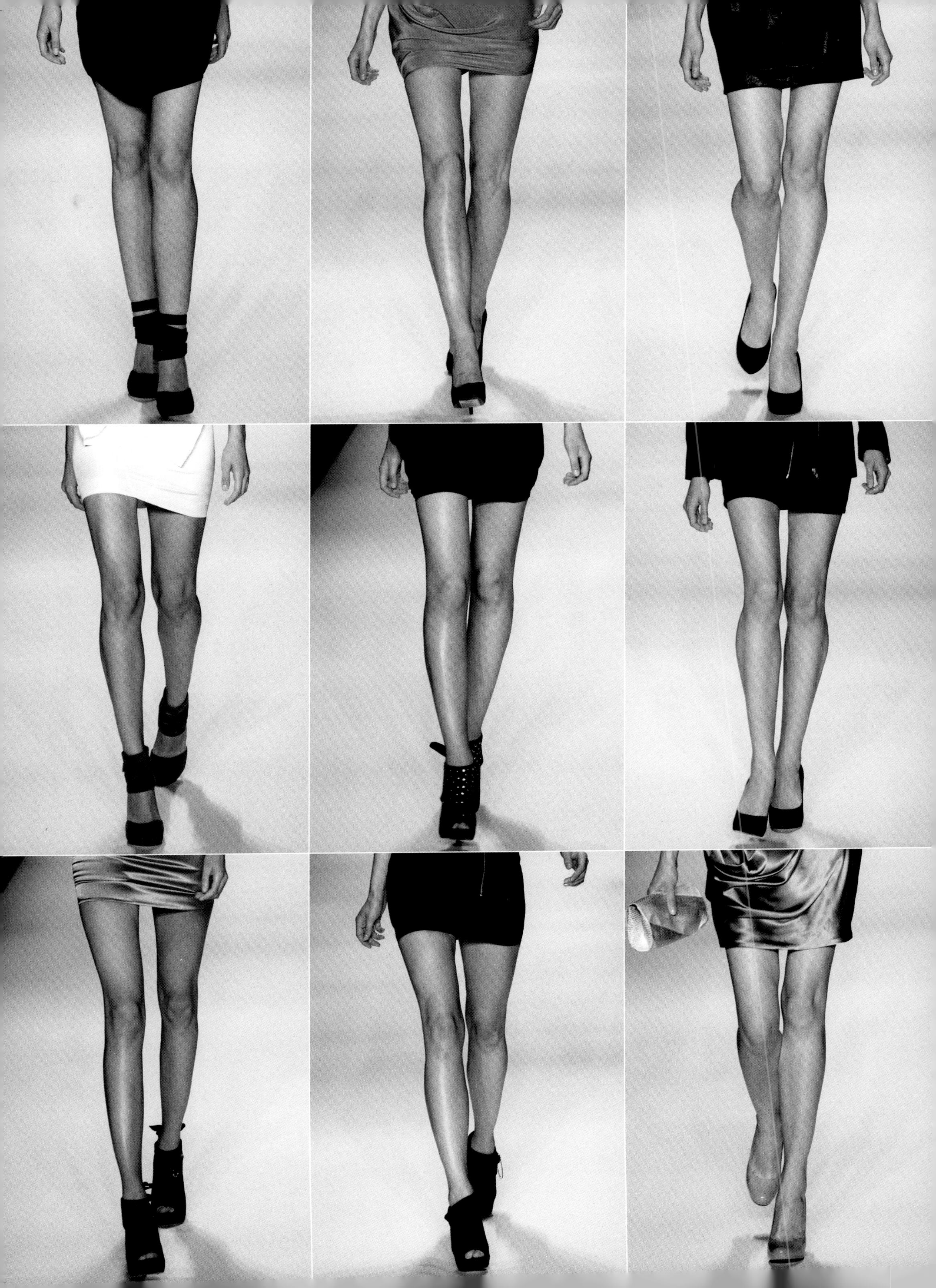

INDEX

CLAUDIUS HOLZMANN

Fotograf aus Leidenschaft, mit unendlicher Liebe zum Detail

Nach Ausbildung und Meisterprüfung zog es Claudius Holzmann 1991 von Karlsruhe nach Düsseldorf, wo er die bhp-Studios – ein Ensemble aus Fotografie und Filmproduktion – aufbaute und leitete (mittlerweile cream digital pictures GmbH).

Seine internationalen Kunden – wie L'Oréal, Maybelline Jade, Estée Lauder und viele mehr – vertrauen ihm seitdem die unterschiedlichsten Projekte im In- und Ausland an. Ob Beautyshootings in Kapstadt, Fashionshootings in Los Angeles oder anspruchsvolle Aufnahmen in seinem Düsseldorfer Studio, Holzmann fühlt sich überall dort zuhause, wo er die Möglichkeit hat, mit seiner Kamera neue Blickwinkel zu öffnen. Als exklusiver Backstage-Fotograf der Mercedes-Benz Fashion Week Berlin und als Starfotograf im Auftrag der UNESCO folgt er seiner größten Berufung, der Peoplefotografie.

Als Meisterfotograf ist für ihn auch die Weitergabe seiner Erfahrung wichtig. 1999 wurde er von der Handwerkskammer Düsseldorf zum Dozenten berufen. Claudius Holzmann ist ein überzeugter Teamplayer und auch ein Fotograf, der sich auf keinen bestimmten Stil festlegen lässt. Bewusst schöpft er die Vielfalt der Möglichkeiten und Ausdrucksweisen aus und überschreitet dabei gerne die Grenzen der Norm – jedoch stets verbunden durch die Maxime der Ästhetik. Es gibt kaum ein Thema, das er noch nicht fotografisch behandelt hat, und dem er mit seiner eigenen, unverkennbaren Art das ganz Besondere entlocken konnte.

A passionate photographer with an endless affinity for detail

In 1991, after completing his training and passing his examination to become a master photographer, Claudius Holzmann moved from Karlsruhe to Düsseldorf, where he founded and managed bhp-Studios (now called cream digital pictures GmbH), a photography and film production group.

Since that time, his international clients, such as L'Oréal, Maybelline Jade, Estée Lauder, and many more, have entrusted him with a wide variety of projects at home in Germany and abroad. Whether shooting beauty in Cape Town, fashion in Los Angeles or sophisticated photos in his studio in Düsseldorf, Holzmann feels at home wherever he has the chance to open up new perspectives with his camera. As the exclusive backstage photographer for the Mercedes-Benz Fashion Week Berlin and the star photographer for UNESCO, he follows his highest calling: people photography.

As a master photographer, it is also important to Holzmann to share his experience. In 1999, he was appointed lecturer by the Düsseldorf Chamber of Small Industries and Skilled Trades. Claudius Holzmann is a dedicated team player and also a photographer who does not allow himself to be pigeon-holed to a certain style. He intentionally explores the full range of possibilities and forms of expression and likes to go beyond the limits of what is considered normal, yet he always adheres to the principle of aesthetics. There is hardly a subject that he has not addressed in his photography and whose special qualities he has not been able bring out with his unique, unmistakable style.

www.claudius-holzmann.de

cream digital pictures GmbH
Berliner Allee 57
40212 Düsseldorf

www.creampictures.com

Photos page 6 © Michael Link, page 7 © Katja Kuhl

Design by Silke Braun
Editorial coordination by Arndt Jasper, teNeues Verlag
Production by Sandra Jansen, teNeues Verlag
Color separation by ORT Medienverbund, Krefeld
Translations by Jane Wolfrum (English), Dr. Anne Emmert (German)

Published by teNeues Publishing Group

teNeues Verlag GmbH + Co. KG
Am Selder 37, 47906 Kempen, Germany
Phone: 0049-2152-916-0
Fax: 0049-2152-916-111
e-mail: books@teneues.de

Press department: Andrea Rehn
Phone: 0049-2152-916-202
e-mail: arehn@teneues.de

teNeues Publishing Company
16 West 22nd Street, New York, NY 10010, USA
Phone: 001-212-627-9090
Fax: 001-212-627-9511

teNeues Publishing UK Ltd.
21 Marlowe Court, Lymer Avenue, London SE19 1LP, UK
Phone: 0044-208-670-7522
Fax: 0044-208-670-7523

teNeues France S.A.R.L.
39, rue des Billets, 18250 Henrichemont, France
Phone: 0033-2-4826-9348
Fax: 0033-1-7072-3482

www.teneues.com

ISBN 978-3-8327-9384-5

Printed in Italy

Bibliographic information published by the Deutsche Nationalbibliothek.
The Deutsche Nationalbibliothek lists this publication in the Deutsche Nationalbibliografie; detailed bibliographic data are available in the Internet at http://dnb.d-nb.de.

teNeues Publishing Group
Kempen
Düsseldorf
Hamburg
London
Munich
New York
Paris

teNeues